I'VE GOT QUESTIONS

GUIDED JOURNAL

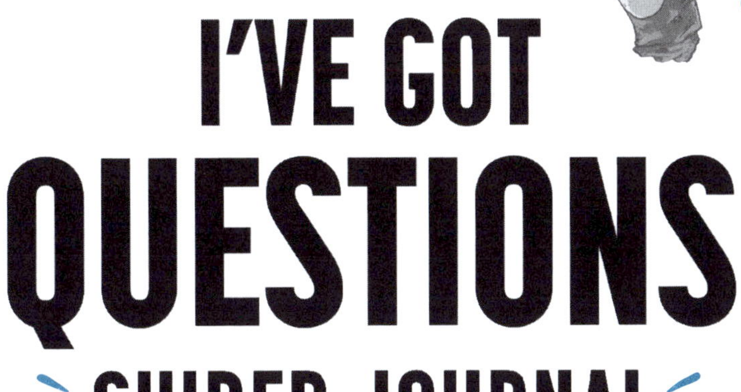

I'VE GOT QUESTIONS GUIDED JOURNAL

PROMPTS AND PRACTICES FOR REWILDING YOUR FAITH

ERIN HICKS MOON

BakerBooks
a division of Baker Publishing Group
Grand Rapids, Michigan

Published by Baker Books
a division of Baker Publishing Group
Grand Rapids, Michigan
BakerBooks.com

Printed in China

ISBN 9781540904096 (paperback)
ISBN 9781493451050 (ebook)

Cover Illustrations by Nate Eidenberger
Interior book design by Nadine Rewa

The author is represented by The Christopher Ferebee Agency, www.christopherferebee.com.

Baker Publishing Group publications use paper produced from sustainable forestry practices and postconsumer waste whenever possible.

25 26 27 28 29 30 31 7 6 5 4 3 2 1

To the original members of the dis/entangle cohort.
Without your wisdom, patience, trust, and thoughtfulness, none of this would exist.

CONTENTS

INTRODUCTION

Out of all the things we manage in our daily lives, our faith is easily putdownable.

That's not a judgment statement; it's the truth. Our lives are full of bills, group texts, kids, appointments, work, meetings, and all the things that sit at the very top of our to-do list in bright red letters.

Maybe you want to untangle your faith, but every time you consider it, a sense of overwhelm befalls you. Perhaps you want to ponder the questions of the universe, but you barely have time to take a shower.

Doesn't it seem like there's never enough caffeine in the universe to keep you awake long enough to think about matters of God, faith, church, and spirituality before you fall asleep?

Faith is one of those things we can put on the back burner, stick to the side, and put a pin in for later. It feels too big, too much, and too unwieldy, and we simply do not have the margin, the enthusiasm, or the time. We know it's important. Of course it's important. Working out our faith and articulating our beliefs are crucial to navigating life. They're how we discern our priorities, choose political candidates, decide where our money should be spent, and orient ourselves in the world.

So, yeah—faith is important, but it's not "You forgot to pay the water bill again and unless you do, we're turning your water off at midnight" important.

In an ideal world, I'd whisk you away from the myriad of responsibilities, tasks, and alarms that make up most of life. I'd pull you away from real life and we'd abscond to some beautiful countryside villa, where a rosy-cheeked woman named Ramona would feed us homemade granola with fresh berries. Tears would be shed, hearts would be mended, sourdough would be started, our connection with God would be restored.

Sounds great, doesn't it? Personally, I would not mind a hall pass from life with its flat tires and termite inspections and panic-inducing news cycles. But escaping from real life is not always feasible. So, we're going to do what I believe is the next best thing.

I wrote the bones of this guided journal in 2021 and led a small cohort of diverse humans through it together online. Single, married, queer, straight, child-free, with kids, old, young. Every participant had one thing in common: they wanted to untangle the knots of their faith.

If you've read my book, *I've Got Questions: The Spiritual Practice of Having It Out with God*, you might know that a controlled burn is a low-intensity fire "started intentionally to clear out overgrowth that might otherwise spark a high-intensity, out-of-control fire later. In other words, it is a fire set not toward destruction, but toward purposeful renewal."[1]

This journal is for anyone who wants to do a controlled burn on the little plot of land of their faith. Together, we will strike the match and watch it burn. We will sift through what remains. We will toss out the detritus. We will leach the soil of its poisons. We will forage for new growth. We will rewild our land and commit ourselves to taking an active role in an active faith with an active God.

There are a million ways you can use this journal (keep reading for more on that). These pages certainly don't contain the answers to the universe or 152 insights into your soul, but they will give you tools to begin the process of asking and working through your questions.

I don't know where you're at in your faith right now. You may not either. Still, you deserve to offer yourself the gift of trying to figure it out. During my own deconstruction, I didn't want a checklist or a rule book. I wanted a friend, someone to help me think through what was churning inside me.

This is me, offering myself as a friend to you.

Let's pick up the faith we so easily put down.

Let's ask our questions together.

Erin

HOW THIS BOOK WORKS

The great thing about this journal is that you can use it however you want. I'm going to unpack some of the options for you here, but don't feel confined by my guidelines. I trust you can think of a lot of different ways this journal can serve you—feel free to explore those options too.

Introvert? Extrovert? Ambivert? We've Got Options for That

You can work through this journal alone, with a small group, or with a partner. You and your best friend from college might text each other your answers. Maybe you and your girlfriend work through a session together. Maybe you do everything by yourself, just you and God having it out. The point is, there's no corral around who or how many people can link up with you for this journal. That's for you to decide.

Busy? No Worries. No Time Constraints Here

No one's going to shame you for not doing a session every day. It's okay if you put this journal down for six weeks before coming back to it. Working through your faith takes time and space; you may need six weeks to process all the questions you have, or to figure out how you'd like to rebuild certain aspects of your faith. Not one part of this is a race, nor will you ever reach a destination. Free yourself from the idea that you'll be able to "Deconstruct Your Faith in Six Weeks!"

Everyone Learns Differently, and We've Accommodated for That

As much as possible, I've woven intentional flexibility into this journal. If reading the guided meditations is difficult for you, scan the QR code on those pages to hear me read them to you. If writing by hand is tedious, feel free to type your answers on a laptop or use the speech-to-text function on a smartphone. If there's an exercise that isn't landing with you, there are alternatives provided almost every time. And you don't have to be limited by what I've offered here either. Maybe you and a friend send voice memos back and forth to each other. Maybe you're a prolific notebook artist, and you'll be creating collages that express your thoughts. Flip through these pages to get an idea of what we'll be doing. You won't need much, depending on how you choose to use this journal, but on a basic level, a writing utensil and some version of a Bible will be helpful.

Organization Is a Helpful Tool, Not a Fundamental Restriction

Each section corresponds to a section of my book, *I've Got Questions*. Reading *I've Got Questions* is not a prerequisite, but I think it certainly helps. Within each section, you'll find breath prayers, guided meditations, mindfulness exercises, question prompts, and more. It's basically everything I wish I had when I was working through my own questions.

Be Honest and Hold On to Hope, Even When It's Hard

It's hard to be hopeful, risk exposure, be sincere, and wear your heart on your sleeve—especially when you've been burned before. But emotionally and spiritually half-assing this journal isn't going to get you very far. Give yourself a chance to be honest, to genuinely engage, and to pay attention.

Decide Your Why

Before you go any further, decide your why. Why are you doing this? Why are you committing to making space for working out your faith? What's the compelling motivation behind putting down other things in order to focus on this? Write your answer down somewhere. Make it into a cute graphic and set it as your phone wallpaper. Get it tattooed. When you sense fatigue or frustration (both completely normal), give yourself the grace to rest, reorient yourself to your why, and pick this book back up. Remembering the reason for your processing will go a long way in reminding you that this is important work, it's worthy of your attention, and you have time.

This journal is meant to serve you in whatever capacity is helpful. I hope it's part of your story of unlearning and rewilding, of making your faith your own.

Let's light this fire, shall we?

THE THINKING BEFORE THE PONDERING

My spiritual upbringing gave me bread. It also gave me snakes. It's taken me a long time to come to terms with both those things being true.

Erin Hicks Moon, *I've Got Questions*

SESSION 1

Faith Cartography

CENTERING PRAYER

Remind me where I came from, so I can better see where I'm going.

A centering prayer is just that: a simple prayer intended to focus you on the task ahead. You can read it out loud, say it in your mind, or write it out. Whatever is comfortable.

If we're going to set a controlled burn on our faith, it's important to know where we got this land from in the first place. Our origins are crucial, because where we come from will influence how we view the world, what we believe about God, our pressure points, and ultimately where we go.

In the first section of *I've Got Questions*, I wrote about how it "seemed to me that when I entered a covenant of faith, I received a metaphorical plot of land. Not big but not small, and this was the place where God and I would be in community together, doing the holy work of trust and love."[1]

That's what we're going to do: we're going to survey the land and map out our faith cartography so that when we're ready to hit the controlled burn button, we know what's at stake.

Let's spend some time thinking about where we started, how we became who we are, and how that affects the way we look at God and faith.

> If it's helpful, go back and look at old journals or photos from your early life. Scroll through those embarrassing Facebook memories. Take your time with this—there's no need to rush it. Interview your friends and family. What do they say? Put this inventory down and come back to it after a couple of days.

The Groundskeeper: Who Am I?

What's important for people to know about me?
When you think about the things that make you YOU, what comes to mind?

You can't understand me unless . . .
This could be a story, a moment, a personality trait, a connection, a song, a poem, anything.

What are my defining life events?

What are the moments that come to mind when you think about the journey of your life so far?

What is my life verse, quote, rule, guiding principle, or mission statement?

Is there a motto that you've adopted for living a purposeful life? A quote that's always resonated?

No matter what, I know this to be true about who I am . . .
This one might be spiritual, or it might be about your character.

Testing the Soil: Where Have I Been?

What is my faith heritage?

What traditions were you brought up in? Was your family open or hostile toward faith?

Who helped me establish my faith in its infancy?

Who first introduced you to faith? Who did you listen to or read or emulate as a young student of faith?

Thinking back on who I was at the beginning of my faith experience, what feelings do I have toward that version of me?

Talk with the younger version of yourself. What's your posture? How do you view who and where you were?

Purposefully Planted or Invasive Species: Where Am I At?

Is there an area or category in my faith where I feel secure or safe?

If you don't feel secure in your faith, that's okay. Explore why.

Who or what influences me in matters of faith?

Who do you read, follow, or listen to in the realm of faith?

Who do I admire or respect on their faith journey? What draws me to their story or the work they do?
This can be someone you know personally, someone you've respected from afar, someone dead or alive.

In *I've Got Questions*, I explain how our unsoothed hearts are our most powerful weapons.[2] In light of that, ponder this question: What unsoothes my heart? What angers me in the world of faith?
Go off.

What beliefs or doctrines am I trying to untangle?

What are you discerning needs a closer look?

Controlled Burn: Where Do I Want to Go?

What part of faith feels complicated to me right now?
What's causing you frustration or cognitive dissonance?

Where do I feel an invitation to lean in?
Depending on your frame of mind around spiritual matters, you might describe this as a "prompting from Holy Spirit" or maybe a posture of curiosity.

What kind of relationship do I long to have with God?

Be honest. Explore what comes up to the surface first, and what you sense when you sit with this question.

When I think about the type of faith I want to have, it looks like . . .

If it's helpful, identify adjectives that resonate with you.

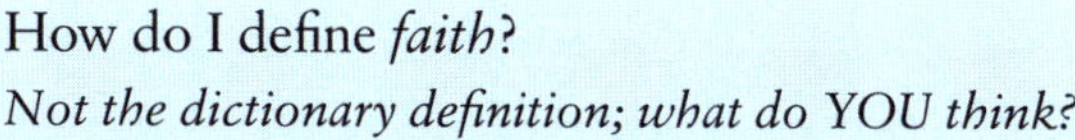

How do I define *faith*?

Not the dictionary definition; what do YOU think?

These answers are for you, to remind you of who you are as you begin this process. You're not a blank slate or a robot or someone striving for perfection; you have a story with highs and lows, triumphs and disappointments, joys and sorrows. Your faith is alive and active.

The purpose of this spiritual cartography is to anchor you to your history, but also to remind you that it doesn't define you. Your story is still in motion, even now.

We own our faith because it's our relationship with God. It's our connection with Holy Spirit. It's our friendship with Jesus. Not anyone else's.

We're all rooted in something, and there are so many ways we can grow. Let's see what that looks like.

WE OWN OUR FAITH BECAUSE IT'S OUR RELATIONSHIP WITH GOD. IT'S OUR CONNECTION WITH HOLY SPIRIT. IT'S OUR FRIENDSHIP WITH JESUS.

NOT ANYONE ELSE'S.

SCREAMING, CRYING, THROWING UP

Ash is nature's fertilizer. When it gets in the soil, it detoxifies and readies the land for something new. Ash and all its attendant grief prepare the way for hope, if counterintuitively. Just ask any farmer who's striking their own match—the controlled burn is clearing the way for something good to grow, and that is the hope that remains even as you watch it all burn.

Erin Hicks Moon, *I've Got Questions*

A Liturgy for Lament

I'm crying because you said I could trust you.
I'm screaming because you said you cared.
I'm beating on the door because you said you'd open it.
Sometimes I look around and wonder where the hell you are.
Everyone wants to ring the liberty bell, but I'm pulling the fire alarm.
Under my breath, on a constant loop:

I'm so angry.
Is this how it's supposed to be?
What is going on?

These words of lament are for you.
Because at one time, we did not have this space between us.
This pile of paperwork and accusations and pain between us.
But you've given up control of this story to us.
And, my God, what have we done?

I'm so angry.
Is this how it's supposed to be?
What is going on?

I'm crying because trusting you is like stepping onto an iced-over lake, unsure if the weight of my questions will crack the surface.
I'm screaming because I need to see you care.

Oh, God, I need to see it.
Please let me see it.
I'm beating on the door because I know what's behind it, and if I have to, I'll break it down to see it again.
Amen.

SESSION 1

The Lament Primer

CENTERING PRAYER

Help me grieve so I may heal.

Lament is a revelation. What is not grieved cannot heal.

We are all at a place of spiritual pain, in one way or another. It's possible you've been walking wounded, doing your best to ignore or push through the pain, convinced you'll deal with it at "some point."

"Some point" is now.

It can be scary to dive into your questions, doubts, and tensions because what if what you once thought was true doesn't hold up? What if the promises you once believed in aren't kept?

As we discovered in *I've Got Questions*, the first step to sorting these questions is lamentation. Following our metaphor of a controlled burn, after we set fire to our little plot of land, we end up with a lot of ash. If you know anything about lament in the Bible, you know it has three ingredients: sackcloth, gnashing of teeth, and ashes on your head. But what you might not know is that "ash can be used as a cleaning agent and even a disinfectant. We're wounded, and part of this process is cleaning those wounds to get a better idea of what damage we're looking at. It does us no good to ignore them."[1]

When you have a wound, the first thing you need to do is wash it. Only then can you see the damage clearly. Before you plant something new, you must first clear the ground. In the cases of washing wounds or clearing land, you often need water for that. The tears of your lament will be the water you need for a season of deconstruction and reconstruction. Glenn Packiam brilliantly describes lament as "an appeal to God based on confidence in His character."[2] Lament forms from a place of saying, "You've said you'd do this / be this / embody this, and I need you to pull through."

Modern times and current cultures have tricked us into thinking we can't ever express any kind of negativity, or that sadness will reflect back as a poor witness. But we have so many biblical examples of lament—it's hard not to see it as a way to connect with God more deeply. Still, we have these swirling thoughts, emotions, and gut instincts that we have no idea how to process because we often get caught up in the optics. How many times have you regulated your own emotional or instinctual responses with questions like:

What will people think / how will people react if I . . . ?
Will I be understood?

It's important to honor such questions. We are communal creatures, and we don't live divorced from our relationships with each other. Yet sometimes we allow the perceptions and perspectives of others to dictate our lament. And if that's the case, we'll never be able to tend to our wounds. When we lock lament inside us, what we perceive as the answer to these questions will instead shut us up and tell us lies about who we are, who God is, and what our relationship with God is.

So, we will lament. We'll lay out our pains, our griefs, our anger, our frustrations. And we will ask God to meet us where we are. Because we know from experience that when the world is broken, God shows up to bring mending.

Breath Prayer

Inhale:

Lament is a revelation.

Exhale:

My heart is close to God.

Breath prayers are meant to be prayed by saying the first line on the inhale and the second line on the exhale. You can say them out loud or to yourself.

The Bones of Lament

CENTERING PRAYER

Help me honestly share my griefs so I might honestly share my heart.

Biblical lament is specific in its structure: addressing the complaint to God, airing the grievance, trying to convince or entice God into action, and expressing either confidence or preemptive thankfulness that God will act. Every aspect is important because together they move us through healthy processing, without us shaming ourselves for being humans with human experiences.

Let's break this down:

Addressing the complaint to God: There's a reason people shake their fists at the sky. Being angry or frustrated with any aspect of spirituality—whether that's the church or God or Scripture or the people that make up the system—is completely normal, because it was never meant to be a system in the first place. There is a disconnect between what is supposed to be and what is, and in that gap lives our lament. What changes for those of us who are believers (even if we're hanging on by the thinnest of threads) is that we know where these complaints need to be addressed:

We have seen God work. We have, at some point, seen God move. In an argument with the Pharisees about working on the Sabbath, Jesus says, "My father is always working, and so am I" (John 5:17 NLT). I mentioned in *I've Got Questions* that Ben, my husband, likes to say that God's chest is big enough to beat on. We may not fully trust God with our hearts or minds or futures at the moment, but we can trust God with our rage and our lamentation.

Start your lament by addressing God in whatever way feels authentic to you. If "Dubious Sky Daddy" is as good as it is going to get right now, that works. God is not offended by genuine attempts at connection.

If you want, spend some time in the following Scriptures that give examples of God's people walking through lament: Lamentations 3:19–56; Psalm 6; Psalm 10:12–18; John 16:20; John 16:33.

Airing of grievances: To borrow a phrase from Kendra Adachi, The Lazy Genius, we name what matters.* In the same way screaming or exercising completes our stress cycles, taking the time to name where we are in pain allows us to experience relief at getting it all out.**

Just as a matter of practicality, we can't live in a perpetual state of grief. What if we viewed our lament like an investment, and we carefully chose what we wanted to spend our grief capital on? What each of us laments over will be different depending on our origin story and where we are now.

Think about your specific laments and grievances. You can write them out here, but if you prefer different modes of expression, don't feel boxed in by the space below.

*Kendra Adachi talks about how to be a Lazy Genius in a lot of places, but you can get an excellent overview of the tenets in her book *The Lazy Genius Way*.

**Hat tip here to the wonderful *Burnout* by Emily Nagoski and Amelia Nagoski. In it, they posit that to fully thrive in our stressful lives, we must physiologically complete what they term *stress cycles* to actually get stress out of our bodies.

Call to action: After naming what matters, we call upon God to act. We stand in the gap between knowing that God moves and asking God to let us see the evidence with our own eyes.

In your ideal situation, how is your lament resolved? Who or what changes? What outcomes do you see as a solution? How would you want God to act? What is your role?

Hoping: For anyone who's been heartbroken, attempting to hope again ain't easy. If you've been heartbroken, take a moment to acknowledge those hurts. List them out here and go into as much detail as you need.

Identify a word or symbol of hope to accompany your lament. Maybe you'll find it in the language of your call to action, or maybe it's hidden in Scripture or in imagery that resonates with you. If this feels too tender right now, simply offer a breath prayer (try the one below) or take a walk, paying special attention to how God might be speaking to you.

There's nothing to do with this right now; there is no action step. It's enough to simply sit with your honest and authentic reactions.

Breath Prayer

Inhale:

Lament is the location—

Exhale:

Where God meets me.

SESSION 3

Guided Meditation

The Lament of Jesus

> **CENTERING PRAYER**
> I ask for clarity and a holy imagination to see new truths and perspectives.

There are lots of ways to meditate, but in our case, we're using the practice to see Scripture with fresh eyes. If you're in the middle of sorting out your faith, Scripture might be a tricky spot for you. The hope is that with a new way to encounter familiar stories, you'll be able to shelve old baggage that no longer serves you and come across ancient truths in a novel way.

https://www.erinhmoon.com/lament

Scan the QR code to access a recording that will walk you through this meditation. You can doodle while you meditate or you can share this with a partner. Don't feel like you're bound by the conventions of this book.

Here's how a guided meditation works. We'll read a story from Scripture together and, using our sacred imaginations and sanctified common sense, imagine ourselves within the narrative. We'll think about the sights, sounds, emotions, and perspectives of these stories. The idea is to think about the stories in a new way, so if you feel yourself leaning on a Sunday school answer, stop and try again. You can answer the

1. **Find a quiet place.** I assume you're doing this in some way already, but try as hard as you can to locate a slice of quiet. Stick your kids in front of a screen, retreat to a closet, put on headphones—do whatever you gotta do! Of course, sometimes perfect peace is not possible, so just do what you can; God sees these efforts and honors them.
2. **Use your own preferred learning style.** Big visual learner? Write down your answers to the prompts. Need to hear it? Open your phone and record yourself reading the prompts, then play them back. Need to move around? Leave the prompts at home and listen to an audio narration of the passage while you're on a walk. Figure out how you best absorb the questions and let that guide you in your meditation.
3. **Pay attention, but not judgmentally.** It's not feasible for us to assume we would be "good" at this on the first try, or that we would be able to only think about the thing we're supposed to be meditating on. If you feel your mind wandering, just guide it back gently.
4. **Unclench.** Do you have a resting clenched jaw? Because I do, and I tend to get very uptight if I don't consciously unclench. You may need to unclench something in your body, or maybe even something in your mind.
5. **Pray beforehand.** Ask God to meet you in the meditation. Open yourself up to hearing from God.

prompts out loud, journal about them in the space provided, or you can talk about them with a friend.

Let's go to John 11.

Read through the chapter once in your preferred translation (for guided meditation, I use The Message paraphrase).

As you read, what jumps out to you? Who are the characters you connect with? Who are you confused by?

Read John 11 again in a different translation. It's helpful to read passages in different translations because it will give you insight into all the ways it *could* be translated—which is good practice since most of us aren't Koine Greek or Hebrew scholars.

Now let's imagine what happened before John turned his pen to this scene. What do you think it was like for Mary and Martha as they watched Lazarus grow sicker and sicker? As they sent an SOS to Jesus, the one person they knew could help their brother? How do you think they felt? What about Lazarus? Was he afraid? Anticipatory? Try to imagine the perspective of the story from each of these three characters.

Put yourself in the place of the disciples who were around Jesus when he received Mary and Martha's initial request. Were they shocked that Jesus seemed callous? Confused that he wasn't running to Lazarus's side? Relieved that they weren't going back to a place where they were in danger (John 11:5–16)?

Place yourself in the conversation Jesus has with his disciples when he decides to go wake Lazarus from sleep. Are you Thomas, resigned to the idea that you are on your way to die? Are you one of the disciples trying to talk him out of going? What is your reaction when Jesus says, "You're about to be given new grounds for believing" (John 11:15 MSG)? Imagine walking down the dusty road to Bethany. Is it quiet with anticipation? Is someone asking questions? Is Jesus teaching? Are you having a side conversation with another disciple, trying to figure out how this will work? What do you say? How do you feel?

When Jesus and his disciples arrive, there's a large gathering at Mary and Martha's home. Mourners have come to pay their respects, to grieve with the sisters. Imagine yourself here. What do you see? What do you hear? Can you smell anything? Are you watching the sisters? Are you involved in their grief? Are you busy taking care of the house to take something off their plate (John 11:17–20)?

Now Jesus is on the scene. It's been four days. The reason John is adding that detail is because Jews believed the soul left the body after three days. John wants us to know that Lazarus is very dead; he's not asleep. In fact, he's so *not* asleep, later one of the women will remind Jesus that "there will be a stench" (John 11:39 NASB). The body will have begun decaying. If Mary or Martha held out any hope that Jesus would raise Lazarus in the immediate aftermath of his death, it was long squashed.

Or was it?

Can you imagine being Mary? Or Martha? Can you imagine the grief they are processing? The anger? The frustration? What else do you imagine they are experiencing (John 11:21–34)?

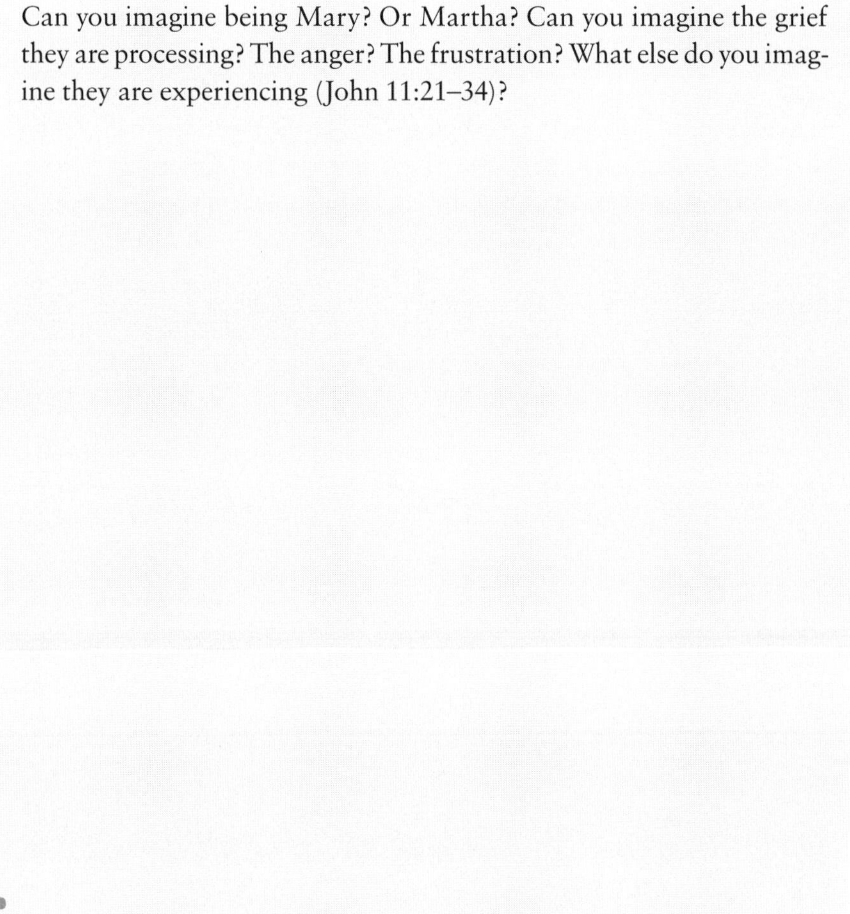

As we near the emotional climax of this story, picture yourself as Mary. In The Message, it says she jumped up immediately when she heard Jesus was there (John 11:29). Why did she do that?

It also says that as Jesus observed her and the other mourners, a deep anger welled up within him. What do you think is the source of this anger? Why is he experiencing it now (John 11:33)? Was it anger that caused Jesus to join Mary in weeping? Was Jesus remembering? Was he thinking about the first death? His own death? Was Jesus angry to have to take Lazarus back? Was it really anger, or something underneath?

Place yourself at the feet of Jesus, weeping and in pain. Place your accusation before him, like Mary did. Imagine Jesus bending low, anger bubbling up, not at you or what you're saying but at the brokenness of this world, at your personal pain. Jesus is weeping with you. Whatever injustice, whatever hurt, whatever burden, imagine him weeping with you. Sit with that for as long as you need. What does that image bring up for you (John 11:34–36)?

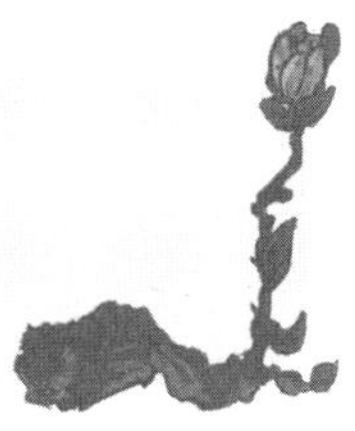

Journey through the rest of this Scripture. Where are you? Who are you? Can you place yourself as different characters? What does each narrative teach you? What snags your attention? What are you surprised by? Something that surprised me is that John *never* explores anything with Lazarus after he is raised from the dead. Why do you think that is? Why is there no "post-game interview" with the involved players?

Linger here. Get comfortable in this passage. Explore the nooks and crannies. Listen to the audio narration via the QR code on page 43 or have the Scripture read to you while you process and immerse yourself in the passage. What other perspectives do you see? Do you need to return to a spot in the story where you felt safe or perhaps uncomfortable? Where do you wonder if God is a part of the story? What are your whys and hows? How does God show up? What does this story have to do with the concept of lament that we've been working through?

Write out your thoughts and additional questions below.

Breath Prayer

Inhale:

Jesus is close—

Exhale:

To what grieves my heart.

SESSION 4

An Airing of Grievances

> **CENTERING PRAYER**
>
> I take what's on my chest and I offer it to you as a cry for justice, peace, and love.

Here, we are writing our own psalm of lament. Really, this can take any form: handwritten, typed on the Notes app in your phone, or a mixed-media collage. Whatever way you choose to express yourself—that works. The idea is to get the lament out of your mind, body, and spirit. But before you do that, let's start off by reading a few more biblical laments.

Read: Psalm 6
Read: Psalm 10
Read: Lamentations 1

As you begin thinking about your own psalm of lament, go back to "Session 2: The Bones of Lament." What are some of the key elements you wrote down? What thoughts surfaced? Do you weep over injustice? Does Scripture frustrate you? Are you questioning whether God is good?

Forge these questions and curiosities into words or pictures for the purpose of stepping back and seeing where you are. The crucial thing here is to remember this is only for you. This is *your* lament. You can be honest. You can say uncomfortable things. It's just for you.

Take this deeper. Write out your lament on a sheet of paper and burn it. Consider the ash and maybe put it in a place you'll see often as a reminder that lament is a crucial part of your process.

Breath Prayer

Inhale:

Lament is an act of faith.

Exhale:

I believe I will be heard and comforted.

WHEN WE LOCK
OUR LAMENT INSIDE US,
WHAT WE PERCEIVE
AS THE ANSWER
TO THESE QUESTIONS
WILL INSTEAD
SHUT US UP
AND TELL US LIES.

HEY, WAIT A MINUTE

Is it possible the questions come not because you're trouble, but because you see trouble? Could it be that you doubt not because you're wrong, but because something is wrong? Are you faithless, or are you faithful to something thicker than empty creeds and heartier than temporary power grabs? Are you poison, causing dissension and division, or are you truth serum?

Erin Hicks Moon, *I've Got Questions*

A Liturgy for Questions

My children begin almost every sentence with "I have a
question . . ."

"Why did God kill the baby T. rex?" she asks one morning after
she brushed her teeth.
"What happens to us when we die?" she asks one afternoon over
ice cream.
"Who that?" he asks, his chubby little not-a-baby-anymore hand
clutching a Jesus figurine.

My children bring me their questions not simply to get answers,
but because I am a safe place.
I am a safe place to hear the hard things.

Behind every question, there is a door.
Behind that door is a room.

Does the arc of the universe bend toward justice?
Can I trust God?
Do you hear me?
Who is my neighbor?
Whom have I in heaven but you?
My God, my God, why have you forsaken me?
Am I loved?
Do I belong?
Who am I?
Who are you?

Our questions are sacred.
Our wonderings are holy.

Grief reveals us, questions refine us.
Our wrestling names us, like our brother Jacob,
we are walking wounded, but the wound is also proof of the showing up.
May we be curious to open the door behind our questions.
May we be brave and pull up a chair.
May we recognize the fear of what might be in the room.
May we settle into the expansiveness of not having answers.
May we honor the mystery of God.
May God grant us peace where we need it, grace where we need it, and truth where we need it.

May our questions push us further out and further in.

May they refine us.
May we never fear them,
for through them is a door,
behind that door is a room,
in that room is Love,
who is a safe place
not to have the answers
and to hear the hard things.
Amen.

I've Got Questions

CENTERING PRAYER

I ask for space and grace to ask my questions.

Start a list of your questions. These can be questions you have about God, Jesus, Holy Spirit, Scripture, church, spirituality, or faith. Think of this as the official record of your questions. We're purging them, getting them out. Unasked questions stay in our brains and hearts, where they can fester into cynicism, bitterness, and apathy.

Jesus exclaimed that truth will set us free, so let's prepare for that truth by examining and honoring our questions.

List out your questions.

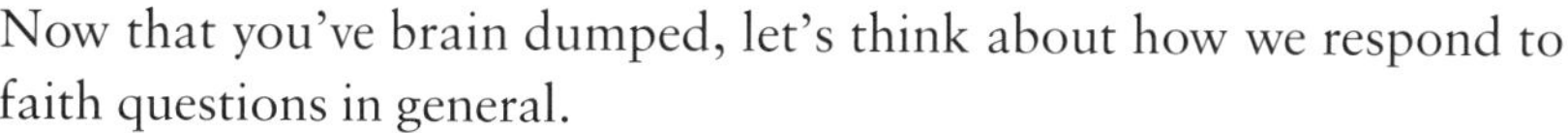

Now that you've brain dumped, let's think about how we respond to faith questions in general.

Are you comfortable asking questions about your faith? Why or why not?

How were questions and doubts—about faith and in general—handled in your family of origin?

Who can you go to with questions about faith? Do you have a person or group that feels safe and open?

Thinking back over your life, can you remember a time when you had a hard question that was answered? What about one that wasn't? How did both of those outcomes feel for you? How did you experience them? Looking back on those times, what do you think about them now?

Breath Prayer

Inhale:

I am questioning—

Exhale:

Because I am paying attention.

SESSION 2

The Patron Saint of Asking Questions

CENTERING PRAYER

Give me the spirit of bold questioning and a soft place to land.

In John 4:1–42, we're looking at the story of Photine or, as she's more commonly known, the woman at the well. The patron saint of asking questions, Photine is revolutionary and has much to teach us.

Let's set the scene: Photine is a Samaritan, which is complicated in and of itself. Samaria and Israel were long-standing enemies due to hostilities that boiled down to the fact that Jews thought the temple should be built on Mount Zion and Samaritans thought it should be built on Mount Gerizim.[1] About 130 years before the birth of Jesus, the Jewish leader at the time led an attack against the Samaritans and destroyed their temple, and in retaliation, a group of Samaritans snuck into the Jewish temple and desecrated it with dead bodies, making it ritualistically unclean.[2] Due to this bad blood between the groups, if a Jew was traveling, he might even take the long way so he didn't have to step foot in Samaria (adding three days to his journey).[3] And if he did go through Samaria, he might be mocked or heckled, sometimes sparking violence between the two groups.

All that to say, the Samaritans and the Jews did not get along.

> It's important to know the backstory of this particular passage, otherwise we miss the impact. Context is everything. If you didn't know exactly how much Jews and Samaritans didn't get along, the renegade nature of this story is diminished!

Read through all of John 4:1–42 in your preferred translation, and then once more with a different translation. What differences do you see? What similarities? Make a notation every time Photine asks a question. Clock your emotions and thoughts as you read.

What's fascinating about this story is that it echoes what's known as a betrothal narrative. Often, stories of engagements (particularly in Hebrew Bible history) begin at a well. Isaac and Rebekah are one example; Jacob and Rachel are another, and John even reminds us of this at the beginning of the chapter, because this was the actual well where Jacob and Rachel met.

What do you think it means that John set up this story to remind us of a betrothal narrative? What would making that connection accomplish for readers?

This narrative contains some teachings about how we can ask questions in regard to our faith:

Photine has a posture of curiosity. When Photine was little, I'd bet she was one of those kids that constantly asked "Why?" This spirit of questioning can often be labeled difficult or frustrating, but Jesus doesn't stop her. He engages with her, showing us that questions aren't off-limits but a part of the process.

She deems her questions worthy. How many times have we swept our nagging doubts and questions under the rug because they seem embarrassing or too vulnerable? Photine believes her questions are worthy, so she boldly asks them. We don't have to be afraid of offending God or stepping out of line.

She's willing to be uncomfortable. Jesus tells Photine some hard truths in this conversation, and she takes them in stride. She doesn't seem to be trying to fool anyone, including herself. Asking hard questions will sometimes beget tough answers. Are we able to face what's true even when it's painful?

She puts what she's learned into action. What's the first thing she does when Jesus shares the good news with her? She tells her people. It's more than likely that Photine was isolated due to her social standing, so it stands to reason she tells people who have defamed and slandered her. Photine was so changed by what she learned, she thought it needed to be offered to everyone, regardless of who they were.

What else can you glean from the way Photine asks her questions?

As you think about the process of asking questions in a faith context, what's difficult for you? What seems as though it would be simple, but turns out it's complicated?

What does this story tell you about the character of Jesus?

What does this story tell you about the character of Photine? How do you want to emulate her posture of curiosity?

Breath Prayer

Inhale:

Questions aren't off-limits.

Exhale:

They are part of the process.

Guided Meditation

Questions at the Well

CENTERING PRAYER

May my questions guide me toward a spirit of truth.

Today we'll be walking through Photine's story and its implications for our own lives.

https://www.erinhmoon.com/questions

Scan the QR code to access a recording that will walk you through this meditation. You can doodle while you meditate or you can share this with a partner. Don't feel like you're bound by the conventions of this book.

Let's go back to John 4:1–42. Read through the chapter once in your preferred translation. Read it again in a different translation. As you become more familiar with the story, what jumps out at you? What characters do you connect with? Who are you confused by?

Now let's think about what happened before John laid this story down. What was life like for Photine as a first-century Samaritan woman? What's her backstory? Why was she alone at the well? What was going through her mind as she walked up to the well and saw Jesus? Was she nervous? Suspicious? Try to imagine what was going through her mind and what her perspective was.

Now place yourself inside the story. We're probably all going to identify with Photine, but why do you? How do her questions feel? How does the conversation go for her internally? The passage makes a point to mention it's noon. Why is that important? What happens in her body when Jesus begins to explain the nuances of her particular situation? What does this good news mean to you, as Photine?

Imagine yourself as a bystander watching this exchange take place. Are you judgmental? Curious? What about when Photine comes to tell you what Jesus has said? What does this good news mean to you?

Place yourself in Photine's shoes. Then place your questions before Jesus like Photine did. Imagine having a deep one-on-one conversation with someone who claimed to be the Messiah not only for you but for a people group that hated your people.

Journey through the rest of this Scripture. Explore the nooks and crannies. What other perspectives do you encounter? Do you need to return to a spot in the story where you felt safe? Or perhaps one where you felt uncomfortable? Where do you see consistency with the character of God? Where do you wonder if God is a part of the story? What are your own personal whys and hows? How does God show up? Where do you wish God would show up? What does this story have to do with the ways we've been unpacking our own questioning? What does it tell you about how God deals with questioners?

You can share your thoughts below.

Breath Prayer

Inhale:

With a posture of curiosity—

Exhale:

I ask God my questions.

Unpacking Our Question Baggage

> **CENTERING PRAYER**
> Give me a posture of curiosity to hold my questions well.

Before we begin, take some time to review and familiarize yourself with the list of questions from Session 1 of this section.

Read: 1 Corinthians 13:12–13
Read: Philippians 4:6–9
Read: Habakkuk 1–3

Take one of your questions and begin digging for the root of it.

Are you curious about why God lets bad things happen to God's people? That question is rooted in God's love and God's justice.

Are you questioning how Christians can look so different from what they profess to believe? That question is rooted in identity.

Go through some (or all) of your questions and find the roots. Are you seeing a theme? Are you surprised by what comes up? If you had to sum it up, what's the overarching message of your questions?

Read John 6:60–69. Place yourself in this moment as Peter. Jesus asks Peter if he, like the disciples who just deserted Jesus, wants to leave because of a hard teaching. Think about how you would answer that question.

Look through your list again. What do you fear? What do you wrestle with the most? What would happen if you got all these questions answered?

The temptation here is to look for ways to answer all our questions. Wouldn't it be wonderful to submit your questions and receive helpful replies?

Unfortunately, that's not faith.

This is the section that never ends. You're not going to get the answers to some of your questions. And the questions that do get answered will be replaced by others.

What we're learning is that God is comfortable with questions. In fact, our questions are often where God wants to meet us. We can wrestle with God because relationships are formed over questions.

Sit with your questions. Keep your list where you can see it—on your desk or taped to the fridge. Add more questions to it. Whisper the questions. Shout the questions. Talk to God about them. Get comfortable with them because they will be a forever faith companion.

If the process of bringing up your questions is difficult for you, try this: split a sheet of paper into two columns. Label one side "Anxieties" and the other side "What If It All Works Out?" On the "Anxieties" side, write down all the reasons you can think of for not asking your questions. On the other side, write down all the reasons you can think of for why it would be a good idea. If it's helpful, talk with a friend who might be able to help guide you in some of your questions.

Breath Prayer

Inhale:

No guilt. No shame.

Exhale:

God meets us in the questions.

WE CAN WRESTLE WITH GOD BECAUSE RELATIONSHIPS ARE FORMED OVER QUESTIONS.

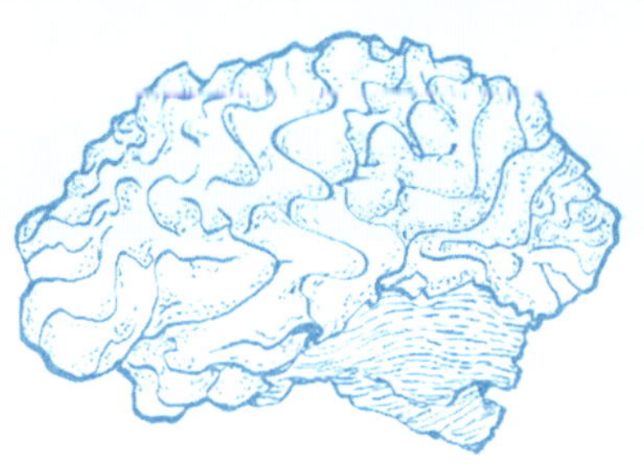

PRESSURE POINTS

PUSHING DOWN ON ME, PRESSING DOWN ON YOU

> Your broken heart, your anger, your rage, your frustration, they're marquees naming what is important to you.
>
> Erin Hicks Moon, *I've Got Questions*

A Liturgy for Pressure Points

God of boiling water and steam-rattled lids.
God of pressure cookers and boiler gaskets.
God of the dinosaur-to-fossil-fuels career pipeline.
From pressure you create—
your hands,
slowly, with your assistant, Time,
working in your own raw materials—
creating still—
creating new things out of the dust.
There are things we must understand in order to trust you (can you be trusted?).
There are stories we need to hear in order to hope in you (can we?).
There are tensions that must be relieved if we are to wrestle with faith in you (do you love us?).
Release our valve.
Help us to hear.
Stay with us until morning, quietly talking in the garden, untangling our pressure points to move us closer to you.
Amen.

SESSION 1

Under Duress

CENTERING PRAYER

I ask for grace where I am tangled, strength where I am fearful, and love where I am hurting.

Examine John 3:1–21, the story of Nicodemus and Jesus. At this point, it's important to understand the cultural and historical context behind the passage, so let's begin there.

Nicodemus was a member of the Pharisees, a religious group with a traditionally bad vibe due to their role in antagonizing Jesus during his ministry. However, they weren't all bad* (the existence of Nicodemus indicates the existence of other not-antagonistic Pharisees).

The Pharisees were the guys who you'd come to with a question about Torah law or what to do about a certain moral quandary. Imagine how wild it is that Nicodemus, a man whose job is to understand prophecy and history from a Jewish perspective, is all of a sudden meeting with Jesus on the down-low.

*We must be careful when talking about the Pharisees to not let our language creep into anti-Semitic territory.

One important aspect of this story is that it follows the passage that details Jesus removing the money changers from the temple, and John prefaces his recounting with the fact that after this,

> During the time he was in Jerusalem, those days of the Passover Feast, many people noticed the signs he was displaying and, seeing they pointed straight to God, entrusted their lives to him. But Jesus didn't entrust his life to them. He knew them inside and out, knew how untrustworthy they were. He didn't need any help in seeing right through them. (John 2:23–25 MSG)

I find this so fascinating: that John makes the clear delineation of how Jesus didn't fall into the trap of trusting his life and value to those who trusted him with theirs. The NET Bible makes this clarification in their notes:

> The issue here is not whether their faith was genuine or not, but what its object was. These individuals, after seeing the miracles, believed Jesus to be the Messiah. They most likely saw in him a political-eschatological figure of some sort. That does not, however, mean that their concept of "Messiah" was the same as Jesus' own, or the author's.[1]

This week, we're going to focus on Nicodemus's pressure point. As we learned in *I've Got Questions*, "If questions are the simmering of a kettle on the stove, pressure points are when the water hits its boiling point, and the kettle starts screaming. And like a screaming kettle, our pressure points are simply too powerful to be ignored."[2] For Nicodemus, he comes to Jesus in the middle of the night and asks for some spiritual grease to work out what he's seeing with his eyes and what he knows in his mind.

Pressure points boil down to trust: "They are the last straw, the final frontier, the fork in the road where we are pressed to decide: Is Jesus really, actually trustworthy? Am I missing something here, or is this issue too important to me to keep going any further?"[3]

As you read John 3:1–21, take notice of the themes of light and dark in this story. What do you think John is attempting to convey?

At first read, what does this story teach you about working through your pressure point(s)?

As you become familiar with the concept of pressure points, what do you sense yours might be? What's the thing (or things) that makes you say: "If I can't get over this, what's the point in even moving forward at all?"[4] If our pressure points in faith indicate the places where we might explode (or even implode), what do you connect that feeling with?

If you're having a hard time discerning your pressure point, you might find it hidden among the questions you outlined last week.

Breath Prayer

Inhale:

Where there is tension—

Exhale:

There can also be trust.

SESSION 2

Surface Pressure

> **CENTERING PRAYER**
>
> I offer to you the places where I'm stuck, where I'm fixed, where I can't move forward. Meet me here.

Read: Jonah 1–4

Jonah gets a bad rap because . . . well, he deserves it. An elitist contrarian with an attitude problem, Jonah is our most begrudging prophet. Still, he has a lot to teach us.

What do you think was Jonah's pressure point? What's the thing that gave him the most trouble in his faith? What did he keep coming back to?

When you read these four chapters, what do you learn about Jonah? What do you learn about the character of God? Where do you see yourself in Jonah? What stands out to you?

Think about your own pressure points. What keeps coming to the surface for you? Where is your relationship with God prickly or frustrated? What do you find yourself stuck in or on?

Consider your relationship with this pressure point: When did you first come upon it? Have you ever thought differently about it than you do now? Have you ever received wise (or unwise) counsel on this point of frustration? Where in your body or mind have you held it?

Jonah also gets mad. Whether or not his anger is justified, he doesn't pretend his pressure point isn't a big deal. He doesn't try to stuff it down or ignore it. We can get mad about our pressure points as well.

What anger or frustration do you feel around your pressure point?

Breath Prayer

Inhale:

I grapple—

Exhale:

And I will not let go.

Guided Meditation

Nic at Night

CENTERING PRAYER

I ask for what you offered to Nicodemus: time to sort through what's important to me and the peace to process it.

We're back with another guided meditation, this time exploring the story of Nicodemus.

https://www.erinhmoon.com/nic

Scan the QR code to access a recording that will walk you through this meditation. You can doodle while you meditate or you can share this with a partner. Don't feel like you're bound by the conventions of this book.

Go back to John 3:1–21. Read through the chapter once in your preferred translation, and again in a different translation. As you become more familiar with the story, what jumps out at you? What characters do you connect with? Who are you confused by?

What else is on the fringes, in the margins? Was Nicodemus anxious about meeting Jesus? What was he thinking as he approached? How did they greet one another?

Now place yourself inside the story: What questions rise to the top when you place yourself in Nicodemus's shoes? How is Jesus speaking to you? How is he looking at you? How is he answering your questions?

Imagine yourself watching this exchange take place as one of the disciples. What are you learning? What questions does watching this exchange spark in you?

What's going through the mind of someone like Nicodemus who is a teacher, knows all the prophecies and predictions, and is seeing the hopes of generations come to pass in front of his eyes? Imagine Nicodemus's heart rate as the truth begins to dawn on him. What happens when Nicodemus leaves his meeting with Jesus? Where does he go? What's on his mind? Who will he tell? What changes?

Journey through the rest of this Scripture. Explore the nooks and crannies. What other perspectives do you encounter? Do you need to return to a spot in the story where you felt safe? Or perhaps one where you felt uncomfortable? Where do you see consistency with the character of God? Where do you wonder if God is a part of the story? What are your own personal whys and hows? How does God show up? Where do you wish he would show up? What does this story have to do with the ways we've been unpacking our own pressure points? What does it tell you about how God deals with those of us under pressure?

Breath Prayer

Inhale:

When you reveal truth—

Exhale:

May I clearly see it.

Counterbalances to Pressure

CENTERING PRAYER

Anchor me in your love.

In *I've Got Questions*, we talked about how the brain is "really just not interested in changing its mind about anything. Call it efficient, call it lazy, but it's very content to keep firing those synapses in the settled grooves it has been creating over time. . . . The work of creating new neural pathways? No thanks, we're good."[1] It is difficult to change your thinking on something you've held deeply—and this includes pressure points. The best way to bring a counterbalance is by making a new groove altogether, and we're going to do that with an anchor mantra.

An anchor mantra is something that you can think, pray, whisper, scream, cry, or laugh through when you need reminders of what you know but cannot understand to be true. Often, these pressure points are so embedded that to consider alleviating them feels borderline heretical.

We don't want to get rid of the pressure point. Instead, we want to give it a place to feel heard. The best way to do that is to let it talk. Like breath prayers and proverbs, the anchor mantra will quickly speak back to your pressure point, reminding you of what is true.

Here's an example:

Maybe your pressure point is hell. You can't get around the concept of hell and why a loving God would send people into eternal conscious torment. So, to create space for a conversation with this pressure point, the anchor mantra would converse with a theology of hell. Examples could be: "God is love" (1 John 4:8 NET) or "God does not wish for any to perish" (2 Pet. 3:9 NET). You're not assigning lies or wishful thinking here; rather, you're counterbalancing the pressure point with truth.

Prayerfully enter this space and allow for your pressure point and anchor mantra to dialogue with each other.

What do they have to say to each other? What wisdom can a pressure point offer an anchor mantra? And vice versa?

Anytime a pressure point arises, assign an anchor mantra to it. Explore new theologians to see if they have ideas for how you might counterbalance a pressure point with another interpretation or understanding of an issue. This is a lifelong practice; it's not a onetime thing.

If it's helpful, find a small visual representation of your anchor. It can be a piece of jewelry, a sticky note, anything. Keep it in your line of sight as a reminder when you need to recall your anchor mantra.

Breath Prayer

Inhale:

I am held fast.

Exhale:

I will not fear.

WE DON'T WANT TO GET RID OF THE PRESSURE POINT. INSTEAD, WE WANT TO GIVE IT A PLACE TO FEEL

HEARD.

SEND OUT THE SEARCH PARTY

After you've set fire to the place you called home and you've cleared the land of both overgrowth and toxins in the soil, there comes a time when you will ask yourself, "What *do* I want to grow here?" And the only way to find out is to venture out from what you know into what you do not.

Erin Hicks Moon, *I've Got Questions*

A Liturgy for Exploring Boundaries

Armed with a spiritual machete,
we hack through the brush.
Are you here?
We don our long pants and cargo vests,
a hat to protect us from the sun.
Are you here?
We enter the great unknown,
eyes searching, still nervous.
Are you here?
Out in the wilderness,
Moses found you.
Will we?
We push past the known boundaries,
where we know you are, and survey the land.
We are kicking logs and picking up stones,
looking for you in places we've never been before.
Will you meet us?
Will you build a fire in this dense forest?
Can we follow you out past where the city lights interrupt the
light you made?
What happens when we hear only your voice and the cicadas,
serenading us
with their song of: Keep going, further out and further in.
Pull us back when we run ahead.
Bring us in when we go too far.
Remind us that you've walked ahead before,
and hold our hands as we step into the clearing,
all lightning bugs and thick stars and firelight.
You are here.
Just as you promised.
Amen.

Push Comes to Shove

> **CENTERING PRAYER**
>
> When I press on the guardrail, may I be surrounded by your love.

We've done a lot of demo work, tearing down walls and inspecting load-bearing pillars in the houses of our faith for rot. We've been peeling back wallpaper and patching up holes in the drywall, attempting to get our structure back in shape. While we might still be working on some of those things for a while, we're moving into a new phase—dreaming about what could be. Because, before we start growing new flowers and tending new soil, we've got to figure out what we want this land to look like. Perhaps a foraging trip is what we need—exploring the edges of faith where we've hesitated to wander.

From the very beginning, we've been exploring with God. God pushed Abraham out even further and made him the father of a nation. Even when Israel was sinful, God still had a plan in motion for their own new thing. Jesus pushed the Jews into new boundaries, redefining what it meant to be children of the covenant. We went from only high priests being able to enter the presence of God one day a year to unfettered access to God through Jesus. These are all examples of exploring those boundaries and finding something worth holding on to out there in the wilderness. Every time we've expanded the boundaries, we've come away with more intimacy and more access to God.

To do this, we're going to link up with the apostle Paul, looking at some of the ways he explored new faith boundaries as Christianity began to take shape, and what that means for us today.

Read: Romans 3:1–31

Read: Romans 6–7

Read: Romans 10

As you ponder these passages, where do you see God working as Paul expands his own faith boundaries?

Paul spends a lot of time unpacking the ideas of how God is doing something new. When have you encountered Jesus in a way that revealed God was doing something new in your life?

Read through the passages above again, this time noting every time Paul reminds his readers what they used to do, and what has changed. What patterns do you see emerging?

What ideas about God or church or Jesus or Holy Spirit have felt out of bounds? Where do you sense Holy Spirit asking you to lean into a posture of curiosity?

Breath Prayer

Inhale:

I will follow you—

Exhale:

Wherever you lead.

SESSION 2

Theological Flirtations

CENTERING PRAYER

As I go into the wilderness, I know you are with me.

It's time for a field trip. Grab your backpack and portable chargers, because we're going foraging. It's time to push out past where we're comfortable, beyond our little plot of land, and head into the wilderness.

What is out there beyond the bounds of what we've always known? Ancient caves, fresh streams, new colors, unusual plants, peculiar seeds, rich soil? Who else has plots of land out here? What grows in the wild?

As we learned in *I've Got Questions*, "Part of our deprogramming includes realizing God is out here, too, past where the well-meaning and the control freaks have laid arbitrary perimeters. And exploration is not the same as pledging allegiance to a belief system. And belief systems are not the same as loving God."[1]

We'll be identifying a belief we've flirted with (or wanted to flirt with). Maybe it's your relationship to the church, or to a specific church. Maybe it's a characteristic of God that you wanted to believe was there, but you've never experienced. It might be personal to you, or it might be a global issue. You can use the prompts below to help figure out your flirtation.

God is more ____________________ than I ever could have believed.

Something I've always wanted to be true is ________________.

I grew up believing that ____________________, but now I don't know.

When I think about ______________________________, I feel ____________________ in my body.

I've always wanted to explore ______________________, but it scares me.

If I embrace ______________________, ____________________ will happen to my faith.

When I pray about ___________________________, I receive ____________________ as an answer.

I understood Scripture one way, but now I'm rethinking _________ ___________________ and the way it was presented to me.

These verses (____________________) seem at odds with each other. Which do I believe? Can both be true at the same time?

________________________ has always seemed to me like a slippery slope, but now I'm not so sure.

I was told that ________________________, but as I've been learning more, I'm wondering if ________________________ is actually true.

Now read Acts 10. Rob Bell has a lovely insight on these verses and Peter's experience in his book *What Is the Bible?*:

> It's possible to resist the very growth and change and expanding consciousness that God desires for you by appealing to your own religious convictions. . . . New stages of growth, maturity, and consciousness bring with them greater freedom, inclusion, and complexity.[2]

Peter knew one thing, had a vision, and then his understanding was completely different when he came back. Bell calls these moments "disruptions" and sees them as catalysts for growth.[3]

On our field trip, we are simply asking God to meet us in the disruptions. The story of Peter is proof that God can do new things in old places, so be unafraid of this exploration. Try on some new beliefs that God is nudging you toward. Ask Holy Spirit to bring into your viewfinder conversations and Scriptures and podcasts and books and articles that help you untangle these new beliefs.

As Rob Bell says in the conclusion of his chapter on Peter and the vision from heaven:

> Wherever you're coming from, don't deny the disruptions. Don't panic when the room spins, because you've seen something real and life-giving and beautiful and good and hopeful that doesn't fit into any of your boxes. It's okay. You're not the first. That's how it works. That's how we grow.[4]

Something important to note about this story: No one was deciding willy-nilly to change the dietary laws. There are clues in this story that show us some parameters around how we might explore our own boundaries:

1. **Cornelius's vision came with instructions.** It's interesting that the angel of the Lord didn't bother to explain itself to Cornelius. It left the remainder of what God had to work in Cornelius's life up to Peter. Everyone had to be in spiritual sync with God for this boundary exploration to be successful.
2. **These visions came during prayer.** The reference to three o'clock in the afternoon hints at Cornelius praying during one of the daily prayer times for Jews, and of course, Peter was praying during his vision. It also came while he was hungry and waiting for lunch, but most importantly, it came during prayer. Peter's commitment to spend dedicated time with God played a crucial role in him being able to listen to and enact what he heard.
3. **There was no agenda until God revealed it.** The angel of the Lord didn't tell Cornelius what Peter would share with him. Peter didn't know that his vision was related to what Cornelius needed to understand. It was only when the two of them got together that they were able to confirm that God was doing something new.
4. **The boundary expansion was accompanied by a life change.** The Romans in Cornelius's house immediately received Holy Spirit, and Peter baptized them. Church tradition has Cornelius becoming a bishop, and while we don't know the veracity, we do know the Romans experienced a miracle after becoming the first gentile converts to what would be known as Christianity.
5. **They weren't left to figure it out on their own.** Not only did Peter enter Cornelius's home and share the good news with all who

were there, he ended up staying, presumably to teach and encourage. This event became the first of many stories about how God was doing a new thing, and how the gospel is open to everyone.

Write out a prayer, asking God to specifically meet you in the place you want to go. What would be helpful for you as you explore?

What questions or doubts or self-talk emerge as you hold on to this new belief or thought or process?

What truths are you uncovering in this story about your own boundary exploration?

Peter and Cornelius made themselves available to hear God. How are you doing that in your own life?

Name your feelings, thoughts, emotions, reservations, fears, and concerns surrounding your boundary exploration. What are you noticing? How are you processing it?

Breath Prayer

Inhale:

I follow disruptions—

Exhale:

To find you waiting.

SESSION 3

Guided Meditation

Divine Field Trip

> **CENTERING PRAYER**
>
> Surround me with peace as I venture out to find the realness of you.

While we're backpacking in the wilderness, we're going to go through the story of Paul's conversion. What could have caused a man so deeply entrenched in and committed to the cause of eradicating Jesus from Judaism to expand that narrow definition of what he understood to be true?

https://www.erinhmoon.com/divine

Scan the QR code to access a recording that will walk you through this meditation. You can doodle while you meditate or you can share this with a partner. Don't feel like you're bound by the conventions of this book.

Let's start in Acts 7, which is not actually Paul's conversion, but it is one of the seeds that eventually bloomed into his conversion. Read through this chapter in your preferred translation and begin asking: What jumps out at you? What do you notice? Who do you notice?

At the beginning of the next chapter, it's going to be revealed that Paul is among those listening to Stephen. Imagine what he, a deeply devout Jew, thinks about these ideas Stephen has about the Messiah. What would they stir up? Where are you connecting to the story? Who is confusing to you?

Go into Acts 8:1–3, then 9:1–32. Try to put yourself in the shoes of each character—even those on the outskirts. What did the disciples think? How did Paul process what was happening? What did Jesus sound like? Was Ananias afraid? What was his conversation like with Paul? With God? What was it like for him to watch Paul's scales fall off? What about the women in the house who would be witnesses as well? What did they experience? How did it change them?

Place yourself in that meeting of the disciples when Barnabas presented Paul to them. What went through their minds? How did they reconcile this change? Imagine Paul's emotions when he explains his transformative experience. What do you say? How do you feel? What are you thinking? What are the smells? The tastes? What can you hear?

Journey through the rest of this Scripture. Where are you? Who are you? What can you learn from each character's perspective? Explore the nooks and crannies to further immerse yourself. Get your thoughts and observations down on paper. What themes do you notice? What places does God show up in that might not be obvious in this story? Where do you see connections with our theme this week of exploring boundaries?

Breath Prayer

Inhale:

I will be open—

Exhale:

To where you are leading.

SESSION 4

Personal Boundaries

> **CENTERING PRAYER**
>
> I find you where they say you do not go. You are all around me.

Today and the rest of the week, take some time to work through those ideas or principles or character traits of God that seem out of bounds. Swim in Scripture. Journal. Pray. Go get coffee with a friend or family member. Engage in the wrestling.

Please know there is no timeline on this. Just because we will be moving onward to our last week doesn't mean you have to have a perfectly curated list of beliefs. We're doing some intricate surgery on the tissue that connects us to God, so rushing is not the answer.

It's also important that you know that just because you've explored these boundaries does not mean you have to adhere to them. It might mean you come back to them later. It might mean they weren't ever going to be a part of your long-term story. In fact, it's possible your explored boundary is something to let go of. Though deeply personal, we can hold these things loosely.

You might need to rephrase or skip some of these questions. That's okay!

What is my explored boundary?

What have I seen, experienced, felt, understood, learned, or heard that has helped me either acclimate myself to this belief or detach myself from it?

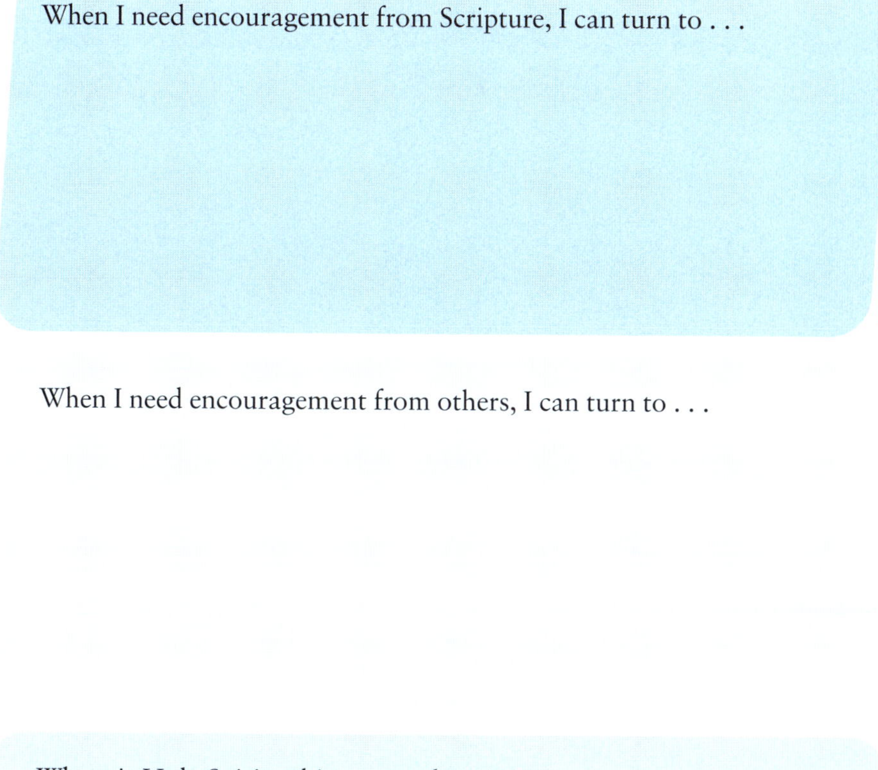

When I need encouragement from Scripture, I can turn to . . .

When I need encouragement from others, I can turn to . . .

Where is Holy Spirit asking me to lean in?

What is Holy Spirit asking me to let go of?

What kind of change have I experienced?

What will I do with my change?

How will my life look different?

How will my life stay the same?

How has God met me?

What have I discovered?

My spiritual director once led me through an exercise where I explained how it felt to me to step out into beliefs I was afraid of. I described being out on an iced-over lake, unsure if it would support my weight. I described pushing down and wondering what would bubble up to the surface. She asked me to work through those metaphors. What happens if the ice breaks? Can I swim? Who is on the shore? Where am I headed? How am I safe? What are the best- and worst-case scenarios?

As you work through the prompts above, take some time to work through your own metaphor of how it feels to explore in this way. If metaphors aren't your thing, you can borrow mine or use your sacred imagination to come up with a different way.

Breath Prayer

Inhale:

I come to the wild—

Exhale:

I meet you here.

WHAT IS OUT THERE
BEYOND THE BOUNDS
OF WHAT WE'VE
ALWAYS KNOWN?

MAKING PEACE

COSMIC FRIENDSHIP BRACELETS WITH GOD

Would it be enough for me to accept that, like everyone else who has ever graced the surface of this planet, I am a beloved child of this God of love? And that simple yet transcendent truth might rip through any notion I had about being right or wrong or better or worse and allow me to live with a heart attuned to the hopes of others and the presence of God? Is this what he meant by "my yoke is easy, and my burden is light"?

Could it really be that simple?

Could we really be that delusional?

Could that offer peace in all our tension?

Erin Hicks Moon, *I've Got Questions*

A Liturgy for Making Peace

Two cords.
Disconnected.
Two halves.
One cord:
The love we bear for God,
the love God bears for us,
the joy of our salvation,
the hope of our brother Jesus.
The other cord:
The doubts and questions that keep us up,
the agitation of our spirits,
the unease we feel,
the pressure points where we might break.
Two cords.
Both a part of what it means to have faith.
But still disconnected.
Two cords.
Picking them up, God pulls them together.
What strains our muscles comes easily for God.
Two pieces of our great cord,
stretching and tightening.
The hands that smoothed knots from wood
coaxes our knots together gently and with purpose.
Ties our pieces together.
For all of it matters.
All is a part of a greater whole.
One rope.
With a knot in the middle.
Bringing us together.
Making peace where we find strife.
Making connections where we cannot see.

This knot won't slip; it is well-crafted.
May we follow the threading of it,
certainties and doubts, hopes and fears,
    looping over and back again,
bound up together, woven and strong.
One rope with a knot in the middle.
Amen.

SESSION 1

The Peace of Wild Things

CENTERING PRAYER

Peace I ask for, true peace that gives me inner rest in my soul.

We've been wrestling and grappling and struggling. And all of that is natural, part of an active faith, part of our heritage of faith. But within that wrestling, there is also an invitation to peace.

The peace extended here is not about tuning out the bad things that happen or faking smiles. It's not ignorance or burying your head in the sand. The true peace offered by God is what keeps you going, what holds you up. It's what pushes you forward and comforts you. It centers you in the midst of tempestuous chaos.

This week, we'll be reading the book of Job. By taking it in small chunks, we'll be able to see the full process of someone dealing with questions, anger, and doubts about God and his people. Like all our other biblical models thus far, Job has a lot to teach us about how we move through grief, questions, and pressure points, and into a place of peace.

Since we'll be reading about eight chapters a day (pro tip: The Message is your friend), our reflection time will be shorter than usual.

Read: Job 1–8

What do you notice in this story? If you've read it before, what's something new you haven't caught before?

What characters do you connect with? Why?

As you reflect on your own journey, where do you see threads of peace?

Breath Prayer

Inhale:

Within my questions—

Exhale:

Peace is possible.

Peace That Surpasses Understanding

CENTERING PRAYER

I ask for comfort in my affliction, I ask for relief in my pain, I ask for rest in my agitation.

Is peace simply the absence of trouble? Is it financial stability or having margin in our lives? What would allow us to live at peace with our questions? Our pressure points? Our anger?

As you read Job 9–17, consider these questions and the ones below.

What surprises you about Job's processing?

What do you admire about how Job moves through this narrative? What seems far-fetched or out of place?

We're also getting a close view of Job's friends. Who do you recognize as someone you've been or someone who has been with you through your own process?

Do you see yourself in Job's search for peace? Why or why not?

What questions do you hear Job asking that articulate this search?

We've been talking about deep peace, but there are also things that offer easy peace: experiencing nature, being with loved ones, and sharing a meal, just to name a few. Make a plan to do one of those things and clock your posture throughout and after. How did it make you feel? What did you experience in your body?

What's a way you can transfer that easy peace to your search for deep peace with God?

Breath Prayer

Inhale:

Peace is a process.

Exhale:

Be with me as I move toward it.

SESSION 3

Guided Meditation

Peace Be with You

> **CENTERING PRAYER**
>
> The peace of God is ever with me. I hold it in my heart like a flame.

The fact that the book of Job made it into the Bible is truly incredible, because it contains so many truths and understandings about God that are frequently overlooked.

https://www.erinhmoon.com/peace

Scan the QR code to access a recording that will walk you through this meditation. You can doodle while you meditate or you can share this with a partner. Don't feel like you're bound by the conventions of this book.

Read through Job 18–25, once in your preferred translation and once in another translation. What do you notice right away? Where does one translation illuminate an insight that you might not have caught with another?

What characters do you connect with? Who are you confused by? Who frustrates you? Do you relate to any of their thoughts or ideas?

Place yourself in the shoes of each speaker. What happens in your body as you read their responses? What about Job's monologues—how do his questions feel?

Imagine watching this exchange take place. Are you judgmental? Curious? Who do you want to shush and who do you want to give a stage to?

What threads of peacemaking do you see appearing in this reading? How do they inform your own process of peacemaking?

Highlight or rewrite the words, phrases, or sentences that stick out to you.

Journey through the rest of this Scripture. Explore the nooks and crannies. What other perspectives do you encounter? Do you need to return to a spot in the story where you felt safe? Or perhaps one where you felt uncomfortable? Where do you see consistency with the character of God? Where do you wonder if God is a part of the story? How does God show up? Where do you wish God would show up?

Where are you seeing Job make peace with God? With his friends? With himself?

Breath Prayer

Inhale:

Not backing off, not letting go—

Exhale:

I ache for God's peace.

SESSION 4

Shalom for You

> **CENTERING PRAYER**
>
> My soul longs for a truce between my head and my heart. Give me deep shalom in my spirit.

Let's explore one of the most oft-quoted ideals of Scripture: Peace that surpasses understanding. Usually, this peace is referenced when bad things happen to us. Let's step into Philippians 4:6–8 and see what "peace of God that surpasses understanding" really means and what it has to do with Job (v. 7 NET).

All the philosophers of Paul's era talked a big game about peace, worry, anxiety, and harmony. The Stoics had an underlying ideology that if you could eradicate worry from your life, you'd be pretty much good to go. Here's a sample:

> Cease to hope and you will cease to fear. (Seneca)
>
> When I see an anxious person, I ask myself, what do they want? For if a person wasn't wanting something outside of their own control, why would they be stricken by anxiety? (Epictetus)
>
> The first step: Don't be anxious. Nature controls it all. (Marcus Aurelius)

Everyone agreed that worry could not be helped, but the Stoics loved to say they could overwhelm their own anxieties with the sheer force of their will. This is also a popular thought process for modern times. Self-help mantras have us look within for peace, even if we are tempering that advice with the added help of therapy and medication.

When we dip into Philippians 4:6–8, however, Paul asks us to consider a different way. When any Jew speaks about peace, they are actually speaking of *shalom*, a word so integral to the Jewish experience that it's considered a name for God. Shalom is more than just a relaxed feeling or peacekeeping. Shalom is about the well-being of a whole—a whole body, a whole person, a whole nation. Shalom means being complete, and it's actually bound up with the concept of perfection—an ethos where everything is in its ideal state; an Edenic existence mentally, physically, and spiritually.

Paul would have readily understood that this type of ideal peace is something we strive for, but not something we attain (at least, not this side of the veil, which was unlike the thinking of the philosophers of the day). So he spends a little time teaching how to orient toward it.

The antidote to worry is prayer. Paul comes out strong here—we can hand our worries over in prayer. What anxieties are you facing? What is disharmonious in your life? Have you prayed about it? Let me be enormously clear here: Prayer isn't easy and it's not a simple fix. Just because you've prayed about something does not mean everything is now fine. Prayer is often used as a bandage, sloppily applied so that other people can relieve their consciences about a problem you might have. Prayer is not neat, but it *is* one of our antidotes to worry.

God's shalom is a guard. Ancient Jews saw the concept of shalom as a divine manifestation of grace. I mentioned that it is also a name for God, and Paul would have had these ideas at the ready. Even the promised Messiah was called Shalom, which makes Paul's statement about how God's peace will guard your heart and your mind in Jesus Christ provocative. He was linking the name of God, Shalom, with Jesus.

We work with God for shalom. Shalom was the work of an ancient Jew's life, and as believers, it is also ours now. Paul reminds us how shalom can be ours with what we think—whatever is true, honorable, just, pure, pleasing, or commendable. This is what Paul wants us to attune our minds toward. Please hear me. Not one character of this is meant to be simple or easy. We hear a lot today about the difference between peacekeeping and peacemaking. Paul isn't prescribing platitudes to get rid of your anxiety-fueled thoughts. He's saying this is work.

With this in mind, let's go to Job 26–32 and see where we might find Job in alignment with Paul's thoughts on peace. How does he do the delicate work of untangling the knots and working with God to bring shalom?

How can we, like Job, come alongside God in our places of discord and strife, whether internal or external, and carry and create that shalom with us everywhere we go?

Where, to paraphrase Frederick Buechner, does the calling God has placed in your heart meet the deep need of the world as a whole?[1] How can you use that framing to explore the boundary lines of true shalom, that abundant life Jesus spoke about?

What does it look like for you to embody shalom and extend it to others?

What does peace look like to you in your life?

How has Job's story helped you define the boundaries of peace?

Where are you seeing Job investing in the work of shalom for his own relationship with God? With his friends? With the world?

Have you ever experienced an example of shalom? What was it? How did it make you feel? What did it spark in you?

Breath Prayer

Inhale:

I am a cocreator—

Exhale:

Of God's shalom.

THE TRUE PEACE
OFFERED BY GOD IS
WHAT KEEPS YOU GOING,
WHAT HOLDS YOU UP.
IT'S WHAT PUSHES
YOU FORWARD
AND COMFORTS YOU.

YOU WILL BE THE REASON THIS PLACE IS BEAUTIFUL

I hope you lean into your belovedness—because for all the laments, questions, and pressure points, that is where good things will always grow.

Erin Hicks Moon, *I've Got Questions*

A Liturgy for Rebuilding

I am stripped bare.
Studs exposed,
wallpaper peeled,
wires sparking as they hang dangerously.
You ask, and I answer.
I engage the choice to rebuild.
The drywall goes up.
A paint color here.
We're shoring up the foundation,
we're checking the roof for leaks.
We stand at the threshold,
blond beams with espresso knots in an organized forest
towering before us.
A place to call home.
A place for shelter, for refuge, for the mundane moments that
will define our life together.
We walk through the framework.
You point out areas where we made new fittings.
"Here's where we patched up that hole."
"Over there we added a new room."
This is a home we made.
Are making.
Will be making.
Together.
This is a home with flexible beams, safe for growing in.
A home with reclaimed wood and new hardware.
A home built with careful patience, with tender hands, with
future hopes.

Here are the keys.
Unlock the door.
Throw open the windows.
Rebuild what was destroyed.
And let the soft green ground grow around the perimeter.
We belong here together.
Amen.

SESSION 1

What Peter Knows

> **CENTERING PRAYER**
>
> Help me dream about what rebuilding a home with you might look like.

The point of untangling a necklace is so you can wear it again. The point of renovating a house is to use it as a shelter again. This week, we begin the process of rewilding and rebuilding with someone who gets it: Peter.

Read: John 1:35–42; Matthew 4:18–22; Mark 1:16–20; and Luke 4:38–41

Read: Matthew 14:22–33

What do these passages teach you about the kind of person Peter was?

How do you relate to Peter in the beginning of his faith journey?

What do you think Peter's mindset was when he decided to follow Jesus? How do you think it changed as he saw miracles?

Rewilding is a form of ecological conservation that serves several purposes. First, it restores natural processes to biological environments that were previously destroyed. Following the metaphor, what's a "natural process" in your faith that disappeared or was destroyed?

Second, rewilding aims to increase the biodiversity of the ecosystem. This means fostering environments so old and new plant and animal life can naturally repopulate the area. What have you and Holy Spirit decided to allow back onto your little plot of land? What new flora will grow?

Finally, conservation biologists care about rewilding because it restores the land to health, which serves everyone. When the land is healthy, not only do the plants and wildlife benefit, but the human population does as well. In what ways will you and the people around you benefit from your faith rewilding process?

Breath Prayer

Inhale:

Side by side—

Exhale:

We rebuild.

Restored

> **CENTERING PRAYER**
>
> Recover and rehabilitate my love for you. Allow me to see and feel your love for me.

Sometimes it can be difficult to uncover the humanity of biblical players. They've been so sanitized after centuries of softening that we have a hard time seeing their flesh-and-blood realness. But Peter escapes sanitization for the most part. Full of contradictions and nuance, he doesn't adhere to a predisposed narrative, and he rarely does the proper or appropriate thing. All through the Gospels, we encounter Peter putting his foot in his mouth, letting his temper get the best of him, and misunderstanding Jesus constantly.

I find Peter to be an interesting companion for rewilding and rebuilding because he had his world torn apart very quickly. At the start of a weekend, he witnessed his best friend and teacher hailed as a hero, and by the end of it, Jesus was dead. If the traumatic and public death of his best friend wasn't enough, Peter also had to wrestle with the knowledge that he'd betrayed Jesus in his last moments. Just like Jesus said he would (Luke 22:31–34).

Read: Luke 22:54–62

What initial reactions do you have to this passage?

Peter is a mixed bag. Moments before this passage, Peter cuts off the ear of the soldier who arrests Jesus. He's passionate for his friend. And yet, a few hours later, he denies he ever knew Jesus. What changed in him? Where do you see yourself in Peter's actions here?

Peter mourned his role in the denial. His deep love for Jesus and his desire to be righteous in the sight of God helped him to understand this separation didn't happen to him, but rather because of him. Peter caused the rift. In our rebuilding, we must be honest with ourselves in our questions and laments and hurts, but also the ways we've participated in driving a wedge between us and God. Honesty is an activator for healing. How can you be honest with yourself?

Peter hung on. If there's any mystery in Scripture I need to unpack in heaven, it's this meeting. Peter held on in the dark days after Jesus's death, likely despairing of the part he played. Even still, he didn't give up. Luke 24:34 reads, "The Lord has really risen, and has appeared to Simon!" (NET).* Call it a hunch, call it curiosity, or maybe it was even fear or despair—for whatever reason, Peter didn't run away. He hung on. What might it look like for you to hang on?

In every other moment where Jesus appears to Peter post-resurrection, Jesus comes to Peter. He appears in the locked room (John 20:19–23). He waits for Peter on the shore, cooking him breakfast (John 21:1–14). This first time, however, Jesus lets Peter come to him. Perhaps in this rebuilding season, Jesus is inviting you to come and see. To see that even though your heart is breaking, he's waiting for you in the garden, ready to prove he's alive and you belong.

*Simon is Peter, in case that's confusing.

Imagine you are Peter in Luke 24:34 and you have a face-to-face with Jesus. You're right there with your best friend in the garden, after all the trials and tribulations and anger and pain. You're remembering all the joy and belonging and love as well. All of it bubbles up to the surface as you lock eyes with the impossibility of who is before you. What does Jesus say? What would you say?

Spend some time imagining this scene. Remember that whatever happened in this meeting, Peter did not leave it ashamed or alienated. Peter was restored. He was folded back into kinship with Jesus. We know this because Peter spent the rest of his life telling anyone who would listen about the belonging found in his best friend. At the end of his first letter, Peter reminds us that God will restore us and make us "strong, firm and steadfast" (1 Pet. 5:10 NIV). How do you see yourself being restored? How are you strong, firm, and steadfast, even among your questions and laments?

Breath Prayer

Inhale:

Your kindness—

Exhale:

Is restoration.

Guided Meditation

Transfigured in Our Hearts

> **CENTERING PRAYER**
>
> Show my heart your glory and teach me to walk renewed by what I see.

Peter saw miracles—he walked on water and his resurrected best friend cooked him breakfast. But I imagine the transfiguration was probably at the top of his list of unforgettable moments.

https://www.erinhmoon.com/transfigured

Scan the QR code to access a recording that will walk you through this meditation. You can doodle while you meditate or you can share this with a partner. Don't feel like you're bound by the conventions of this book.

The transfiguration was an event where Jesus took three of his disciples (Peter, James, and John) up to the top of a mountain to witness . . . well, something pretty mysterious. Right in front of his disciples' faces, Jesus changed in appearance from the man they knew into a being clothed in light.

Let's go to Matthew 17:1–8. Read through the chapter once in your preferred translation. Read it again in a different translation. As you read, what initially grabs your attention?

Who are the characters you connect with? Who are you confused by?

What parts of the story confuse you?

Imagine being on the mountain with Jesus during the transfiguration. What are you thinking? What do you notice?

In your mind's eye, what happens after this moment?

Think about your senses—what do you smell, taste, hear?

As you work your way through this passage, imagine what it must have been like to hear the audible voice of God speak directly to you, while the Messiah talks to Moses and Elijah.

This event impacted Peter so deeply, he wrote about it later in one of his letters:

> We weren't, you know, just wishing on a star when we laid the facts out before you regarding the powerful return of our Master, Jesus Christ. We were there for the preview! We saw it with our own eyes: Jesus resplendent with light from God the Father as the voice of Majestic Glory spoke: "This is my Son, marked by my love, focus of all my delight." We were there on the holy mountain with him. We heard the voice out of heaven with our very own ears.
>
> We couldn't be more sure of what we saw and heard—God's glory, God's voice. The prophetic Word was confirmed to us. You'll do well to keep focusing on it. It's the one light you have in a dark time as you wait for daybreak and the rising of the Morning Star in your hearts. (2 Pet. 1:16–19 MSG)

That image of the one light in a dark time as you wait for daybreak is where so many of us are right now. We are sifting through the dirt to find that one light, something to hold on to in the darkness. It just might be that after the transfiguration, Peter finally understood that Jesus was worth rebuilding his entire faith structure for. Of course, he messed up after this. He missed the mark often. But that one light is what kept him afloat: that image of Jesus as God on earth, and the million little ways he brought God's glory down to those who were sick or dead or poor in spirit.

As you consider this passage, think about your own moment of transfiguration. For you, what moment in time has pulled you back, reminding you that God is who God says God is?

How have you experienced God as you've worked through this process? Where has God surprised you?

What has God revealed to you during this process? What new or old truths have been uncovered that you want to keep exploring?

Breath Prayer

Inhale:

I am transformed—

Exhale:

By your light.

SESSION 4

The Work of Our Lives

> **CENTERING PRAYER**
>
> Give me the strength and passion to honor the work of my life. Sustain me with your love.

Later in Peter's life, he (allegedly) wrote two epistles—1 Peter and 2 Peter—that made their way into the canon of Scripture. It's possible they were written by Peter himself or transcribed through a secretary, perhaps a student of his or someone close to him. Whatever the case may be, these letters give us a glimpse into a rebuilding process that begins at ground zero. Let's see what we might glean from Peter's letters.

Read: 1 Peter 1:3–2:3

Rebuilding begins between you and God. As we've walked through this personal process, I hope it has become clear what you're deconstructing from and just how intimate that is. Peter had to do this as well, as he outlines in verses 10–12. For his whole life, for the life of his entire culture, people thought the Messiah would be one thing, and he turned out to be something completely different. Yet, Peter comes to a place where he rejoices in that, and it pushes him forward to draw closer to Christ.

Read: 1 Peter 3:8–18

Your new life is not like your old life. Things will change when you step back onto your little plot of land. The work of loving others, despite their misunderstandings, their bad theology, and their apathy, is the work of our lives. That little plot of land? It's producing shade and food not just for you but for others as well.

Read: 2 Peter 2:1–22

Let God take care of those who would mislead his people. Just . . . read this chapter and realize that God isn't and never has been unaware of those who would deceive and take advantage of his people. I'm not proud of how comforting this is, and yet it's also a warning for all of us. Peter, a man who followed the tenets of Judaism, who longed for the coming Messiah, had to come to terms with the idea that the teachers he trusted were wrong about some things. Still, even with what he experienced and saw, his life would be spent in service to God.

That is what real deconstruction and reconstruction will give you: The gift of knowing God isn't easily understood, but God is real. God is not a theory or a prophecy. God is incarnate, God is bending down, God is here. We do not have to comprehend it to make it true. Can we trust the God of rewilding and rebuilding to pull love and hope from the ground of our heart, even in our unknowing? Even in our disbelief?

I hope that when you've finished going through this process, that is what you come away with. A renewed vision of who God is and God's deep care and love for you. The understanding that we all know so little, but what we are certain of is secure.

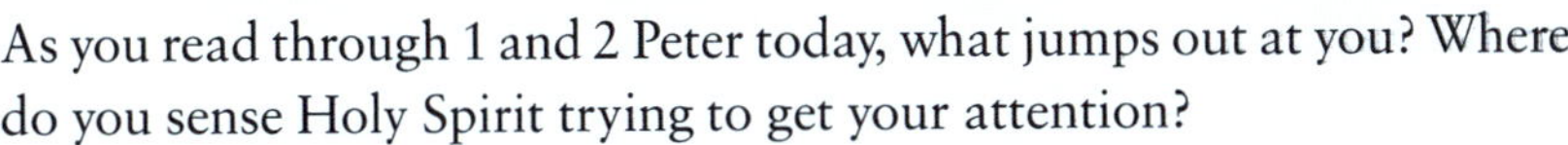
As you read through 1 and 2 Peter today, what jumps out at you? Where do you sense Holy Spirit trying to get your attention?

In your faith exploration, what are you finding to be the most difficult parts? Where are you getting hung up?

As you begin to look back on this process, what emerges for you? More questions? More doubts?

If you could write or whisper a prayer to honor this place you've come to, what would you say? What would you want God to know?

Breath Prayer

Inhale:

You are here with me—

Exhale:

In the renovation.

PERHAPS IN THIS REBUILDING SEASON, JESUS IS INVITING YOU TO COME AND SEE. . . . HE'S WAITING FOR YOU IN THE GARDEN, READY TO PROVE HE'S ALIVE

AND YOU BELONG.

CONTINUING ON

What Happens Now?

This is not the end.

What you're left with at the end of this experience is, more than likely, not a neatly wrapped narrative where you're "finally okay" or "better." It's possible you close this journal with more questions than you started with. Maybe you didn't get as many knots untangled as you would have wanted.

That's okay. Let me tell you why.

Our faith is not a straight line with a final destination. Visually, it's more like a child scribbling—long straight lines that descend into furious tangles. The thing about faith is that it's living and active. You are never done. You might double or triple back on something you thought you left long ago. You might have long seasons of simple contentment, but our faith is the work of our life, and it doesn't end until we do. We come alongside God in this work, because that is the whole point.

I have one final invitation for you as a way to mark this time in your life: Write a letter to God. Talk about these changes and tender spots. Ask God for things: a fresh start, a paid bill, a new job, a repaired relationship. Push past the inclination to write this off as corny. Speak to God in the familiar tones you save for friends and family. Share what you've learned, how you've changed, the ways you've grown.

You've done the work with fear and trembling, but don't stop. Keep pushing to connect deeper. To ask questions. To be tender. To grab hold of the hem of Jesus's robe. Now is the time to stand in the middle of your little plot of land, side by side with the great Rebuilder, and enjoy the fruit of what you've planted.

Breath Prayer

Inhale:

Nothing can separate me—

Exhale:

From your love.

ACKNOWLEDGMENTS

I want to thank everyone at Baker Books, especially Brianna, Brian, Nate, Shelly, Chris, Lauren, and Erin. Y'all are genuinely amazing as humans and book wizards, and I'm really grateful my first foray into publishing was with such an exceptional team.

If I was in charge of awarding Presidential Medals of Freedom, Jonathan Merritt would be first on the list for excellence in agenting and personing.

Rachel Marie Kang edited this puppy, and while editing feels like water torture, she made it delightful. I bend the knee!

I would not be a functioning human without Hannah Gregg. Full stop. I am enormously appreciative to her for all the ways she keeps my head on straight and helps me manage my life. She is indispensable to me.

So many of my friends and family members helped form what you read in this journal; it's through years of conversation and working out our faith together that you hold it in your hands. Thank you for always being willing to sit with questions and hold space for mystery.

And thank you, reader, for trusting me and sharing your thoughts within these pages. It's no small thing and it means the world to me.

NOTES

Introduction

1. Erin Hicks Moon, *I've Got Questions: The Spiritual Practice of Having It Out with God* (Baker Books, 2025), 44.

Faith Cartography

1. Erin Hicks Moon, *I've Got Questions: The Spiritual Practice of Having It Out with God* (Baker Books, 2025), 35.
2. Moon, *I've Got Questions*, 163.

The Lament Primer

1. Erin Hicks Moon, *I've Got Questions: The Spiritual Practice of Having It Out with God* (Baker Books, 2025), 71.
2. Glenn Packiam, "Five Things to Know About Lament," N. T. Wright Online, April 3, 2020, https://www.ntwrightonline.org/five-things-to-know-about-lament.

The Patron Saint of Asking Questions

1. Flavius Josephus, *Antiquities of the Jews*, trans. William Whiston (1895), 13.74.
2. Josephus, *Antiquities*, 18.30.
3. Flavius Josephus, *The Complete Works of Flavius Josephus*, trans. William Whiston (Thomas Nelson, 1851), 485.

Under Duress

1. John 2:23, note aw, NET Bible, copyright © 1996, 2019 by Biblical Studies Press, L.L.C.
2. Erin Hicks Moon, *I've Got Questions: The Spiritual Practice of Having It Out with God* (Baker Books, 2025), 144.
3. Moon, *I've Got Questions*, 144.
4. Moon, *I've Got Questions*, 144.

Counterbalances to Pressure

1. Erin Hicks Moon, *I've Got Questions: The Spiritual Practice of Having It Out with God* (Baker Books, 2025), 118.

Theological Flirtations

1. Erin Hicks Moon, *I've Got Questions: The Spiritual Practice of Having It Out with God* (Baker Books, 2025), 186.
2. Rob Bell, *What Is the Bible?: How an Ancient Library of Poems, Letters, and Stories Can Transform the Way You Think and Feel about Everything* (HarperOne, 2019), 165.
3. Bell, *What Is the Bible?*, 167.
4. Bell, *What Is the Bible?*, 167.

Shalom for You

1. Frederick Buechner, *Wishful Thinking: A Seeker's ABC* (HarperCollins, 1973), 119.

ERIN HICKS MOON is a writer, podcaster, and storyteller who helps people disentangle faith by creating a kind and curious community that welcomes honest doubt and questions. She is the Resident Bible Scholar and host of the *Faith Adjacent* podcast, and senior creative at Podcast Media Group. Her popular weekly newsletter, "The Swipe Up," has garnered nearly twenty thousand highly engaged subscribers, and she has written and produced several popular Bible study guides. Author of *I've Got Questions*, Erin lives in Birmingham, Alabama, with her husband and three children.

Connect with Erin:

ErinHMoon.com